LANGUAGE ARTS 503

CONTENTS

Author: **Joyce Hornby, Ed. Specialist**
Editor-in-Chief: Richard W. Wheeler, M.A.Ed.
Editor: Elizabeth Loeks Bouman
Consulting Editor: Rudolph Moore, Ph.D.
Revision Editor: Alan Christopherson, M.S.

Alpha Omega Publications®

804 N. 2nd Ave. E., Rock Rapids, IA 51246-1759

LANGUAGE ARTS 503

Where did we get words?

How did everything get its name?

Why are there so many languages?

Do you know the answers to the questions above? Most people are puzzled, amazed, and curious when they think about the millions and millions of words man has used since his creation. The story of our language is the theme of the lessons in this LIFEPAC®. In these lessons, you will learn what language is, when it began, and how it changes. You will study the structure of words and how to combine them into meaningful communication symbols.

You will also be given opportunities to practice spelling and handwriting skills. You will have many opportunities to use your gift of language and to share your original ideas in stories, poems, and songs.

OBJECTIVES

Read these objectives. The objectives tell you what you should be able to do when you have successfully completed this LIFEPAC. Each section will list according to the numbers below what objectives will be met in that section.

When you have finished this LIFEPAC, you should be able to:

1. Tell how language was created.
2. Identify details from a reading selection.
3. Select the main ideas of a reading selection.
4. Place the events of a reading selection in their proper order.
5. Pronounce heteronyms correctly, using context clues.
6. Define new words.
7. Identify a complete sentence.
8. Identify the subject and predicate in a sentence.
9. Write the capital letters *N* through *Z* in cursive handwriting.
10. Spell new words.
11. Identify cause and effect statements in written material.

12. Identify propaganda techniques in advertisements.
13. Write a short summary of what you have read.
14. Change the meaning of root words by adding prefixes and suffixes.
15. Identify and use adjectives and adverbs.
16. Identify an author's purpose.
17. Develop a historical time line.
18. Write definitions for homonyms.
19. Express the literal meaning of idioms.
20. Write a descriptive short story.

VOCABULARY

Study these new words. Learning the definitions of these words is a good study habit and will improve your understanding of this LIFEPAC.

abound (u bound'). Be plentiful.

abuse (u byüz'). Use wrongly; make bad use of.

accomplishment (u kom' plish munt). A success in completing something.

appreciation (u prē' shē ā' shun). Recognizing a thing's worth; highly valuing.

authentic (ô then' tik). What it claims to be; real; genuine.

cell (sel). Small unit of living matter.

cobbler (kob' lur). A person who repairs shoes.

confession (kun fesh' un). Admitting one's sins.

creation (krē ā' shun). Act of making something.

disobedience (dis' u bē' de uns). Failure to obey.

entangle (en tang' gul). To get involved in.

environment (en vi' run munt). Surroundings that influence growth.

evolve (i volv'). To unfold; develop gradually.

examination (eg zam' u nā' shun). A test of knowledge.

Germanic (jėr man' ik). Of German origin; relating to Germany.

gourmet (gu̇r' ma). Expert in judging fine foods.

harbinger (här' bin jur). Something that comes before something else and indicates its approach.

helpmeet (help' mēt'). Helper; wife or husband.

monk (mungk). Man who gives up everything else for religion.

nomadic (no mad' ik). Wandering.

opportunity (op' ur tü' nu tē). A good chance; favorable time.

relationship (ri lā' shun ship). Connection; condition of belonging to the same family or group.

revenge (ri venj'). Harm done in return for a wrong.

sacrifice (sak' ru fīs). That which is offered to God.

scholar (skol' ur). Person having much knowledge.

scop (skop). An Old English poet.

squire (skwīr). A young man of a noble family who attends to a knight.

subtle (sut' ul). Sly; tricky.

unacceptable (un' ak sep' tu bul). Not worth taking.

unique (ū nēk'). Having no like or equal; one of a kind.

Note: All vocabulary words in this LIFEPAC appear in **boldface** print the first time they are used. If you are unsure of the meaning when you are reading, study the definitions given.

Pronunciation Key: h**a**t, **ā**ge, c**ã**re, f**ä**r; l**e**t, **ē**qual, t**ė**rm; **i**t, **ī**ce; h**o**t, **ō**pen, **ô**rder; **oi**l; **ou**t; c**u**p, p**u̇**t, r**ü**le; **ch**ild; lo**ng**; **th**in; /*TH*/ for **th**en; /*zh*/ for mea**s**ure; /*u*/ represents /*a*/ in **a**bout, /*e*/ in tak**e**n, /*i*/ in penc**i**l, /*o*/ in lem**o**n, and /*u*/ in circ**u**s.

I. SECTION ONE

Language is the art of communication through speaking or writing. **Scholars** have been curious about the development of language. In this LIFEPAC, you will study the way language began.

Many books have been written about the history of language. Some authors try to explain the story of man and his language without including God. These people tell a story of man's **evolving** from a one-**celled** animal. After millions of years of gradual change, a human being was produced. Many more years passed before man developed intelligent speech. This explanation for the development of language cannot be proven. It remains a theory.

The Holy Bible is the **authentic** written record of God's communication with His **creation** in heaven and on earth. Jesus said (Mark 13:31), "Heaven and earth shall pass away: but my words shall not pass away." This unchangeable record, the Bible, has much to say about the use and abuse of language.

Review these objectives. When you have completed this section, you should be able to:

1. Tell how language was created.
2. Identify details from a reading selection.
3. Select the main ideas of a reading selection.
4. Place the events of a reading selection in their proper order.
5. Pronounce heteronyms correctly, using context clues.
6. Define new words.
7. Identify a complete sentence.
8. Identify the subject and predicate in a sentence.
9. Write the capital letters *N* through *Z* in cursive handwriting.
10. Spell new words.

Restudy these vocabulary words.

abuse
accomplishment
appreciation
authentic
cell
creation
evolve
examination
harbinger
helpmeet
relationship
scholar
unique

A PLOT AND A PLAN MADE IN HEAVEN

Long before the earth was created, God had created angels. Angels were able to both think and speak: they could communicate with one another. Lucifer was a very beautiful and powerful angel. Isaiah 14:12 refers to him as the son of the morning. God created Lucifer for a special purpose. He gave Lucifer the power and ability to do his work perfectly. Lucifer admired himself. He told himself how beautiful, wise, and powerful he was. Selfish pride controlled Lucifer's thoughts, and he began plotting against God. Isaiah 14:12–18 tells the story of this evil plot.

Read Lucifer's goals.

"I will ascend into heaven."
"I will exalt my throne above the stars of God."
"I will sit also upon the mount of the congregation."
"I will ascend above the heights of the clouds."
"I will be like the Most High."

Lucifer shared his plot with other angels. Lucifer's plot did not surprise God, for God knows everything. God knew that Lucifer could not be trusted to serve Him. God cast Lucifer and the angels who were in agreement with Lucifer out of heaven. Lucifer then became Satan. God gave Satan permission to be on earth.

Lucifer's plot teaches us how the gift of language can be **abused**. Whenever a proud, selfish thought becomes a wicked plot and is then communicated to other people, language is abused.

Before Lucifer's wicked plot came into being, God had a plan to rescue man, His prized **creation**. God used language to communicate His plan. In Revelation 13:8, the Bible speaks of "...the Lamb slain from the foundation of the world." This statement tells us about the agreement God the Father, God the Son, and God the Holy Spirit made to provide a Savior for mankind.

The Biblical record proves that God used language to communicate His plan of salvation for man, to cast Lucifer out of heaven, to create heaven and earth, and to have fellowship with man. These facts prove that the power and ability to communicate is a divine characteristic God has graciously shared with His creation. God uses language perfectly, but Satan abuses language. King David prayed (Psalm 19:14), "Let the words of my mouth, and the meditation [thoughts] of my heart, be acceptable in thy sight, O Lord, my strength, and my Redeemer." Make this *your* prayer.

Recall details from the story you just read.

1.1 Answer *true* if the statement is correct as you read it in the story, A *Plot and a Plan Made in Heaven.* Answer *false* if the statement is not correct.

a. __________ Language is the art of communicating ideas through talking or writing.

b. __________ Intelligent creatures, such as angels, dogs, human beings, or birds, communicate through the use of spoken and written language.

c. __________ God has always been able to communicate; therefore, language has always existed.

d. __________ God created Lucifer with the ability to use the gift of language.

e. __________ Thinking is an important part of communicating.

f. __________ Lucifer abused the gift of language when he became boastful about his abilities.

g. __________ Plotting to put yourself in a place of authority is acceptable if you are more intelligent than the person who is in leadership.

h. __________ God's plan to rescue man was made after Lucifer plotted to overthrow Him and become God.

i. __________ The gift of language can be used to express ideas, to correct ourselves, and to share experiences with others.

j. __________ When a plan is revealed to others, people use the gift of language.

LANGUAGE IN THE BEST HOME AND GARDEN

Gardening is a favorite pastime for people all over the world. A beautiful garden is something children love to see. One **harbinger** of spring is the planting of gardens. People talk about how and when to plant their seeds. They watch over them carefully and wait patiently for the seed to grow. After the garden has been planted, the gardener waits for the proper amount of sunshine and rain to make it grow. God must control the weather to make the garden fruitful.

God and man have been gardening since the very first man was created. Genesis chapter 2 tells about that first home and garden. To learn that God's home for man was in a garden that He planted is important. Since your address is the name of the place where you live, we can say that the first man's name and address were

Adam,
Garden of Eden.

God talked to Adam in the Garden of Eden. He told him what he should and should not eat. He also told him what he should do.

God knew that Adam was curious and would want to discover things about his environment. He knew that man would need someone to talk to and make plans with. Remember, man was made in God's image.

Adam had to compare and make a choice. God had created all birds and all animals without giving them names. Giving the animals names was Adam's first task, and it was his first use of the gift of language. God brought all the birds and animals to Adam. Whatever Adam called them, that was the name by which they were known.

What an exciting time it must have been!

Just imagine each animal making its **unique** sound as it walked past Adam. However, Adam noticed one thing after the parade was over. Not one animal looked, sounded, or acted like a man. Adam must have felt very lonesome at that moment.

On that very important day, Adam had no one with whom he could share a great **accomplishment**. God understood Adam's need. He knew that no animal would be able to be a good companion for Adam. Adam was made in God's image; only another person made in God's image could be a **helpmeet**.

God caused a deep sleep to fall upon Adam. While he was sleeping, God took one of Adam's ribs and made another person. What a beautiful creation she was!

God brought that beautiful creation to Adam. When he saw her, he said these words, (Genesis 2:23): "...This is now bone of my bones, and

flesh of my flesh: she shall be called Woman, because she was taken out of Man." These words express Adam's **appreciation** for his lovely wife.

This statement is the first record of a man talking to another person. Adam used language to identify or name animals, and he used language to describe a **relationship** with another person. Today when we test people's intelligence, we give them an **examination** which tells how well they can identify and describe relationships. Language and all of its usages started with the first man in the garden of Eden.

Main idea. Getting the main idea of what you read is a very helpful reading skill. The main idea is a summary of all the details found in a certain paragraph or reading selection. Most of the time the main idea will be either the first or the last sentence of a paragraph. Writers give you the main idea and then write details that support it, or they give you the details first and then summarize the paragraph with a main idea sentence. These two ways are the most common methods of expressing the main idea. Some other ways will be studied at another time.

Select the main idea for the following paragraphs from *Language in the Best Home and Garden.* Underline the main idea you choose.

1.2 Paragraph One
a. Gardening is a favorite pastime.
b. Proper sunshine and rain are important.
c. People wait for seeds to grow.

1.3 Paragraph Two
a. God and man have been gardening since man was created.
b. The first man's name was Adam.
c. Man's home was in the garden.

1.4 Paragraph Three
a. God talked to Adam in the garden.
b. God told him what to do.
c. God told him what to eat.

1.5 Paragraph Seven
a. Each animal made a unique sound.
b. Adam felt very lonesome.
c. Adam noticed that no animal looked like a man.

1.6 Paragraph Eleven
a. Adam used language to identify animals.
b. Language started with the first man.
c. Today we give tests.

Sequence of events. Being able to place the events of a reading selection in their proper order is an important reading skill. This sequencing skill will help you organize your thinking. After you read, ask yourself what came before and after a certain event.

Sequencing is like following the directions for building something. One step must be completed before the next step is begun. The next time you read something, try to organize the thoughts in your mind. If you practice this skill, you should notice improvement in your comprehension.

Place the events in the correct order.

1.7 Write the number 1 in front of the event that happened first in the story, 2 in front of the event that came second, and so on.

a. ________ Adam noticed that no animal looked like him.

b. ________ God created man.

c. ________ God caused Adam to fall asleep.

d. ________ Adam named all the animals.

e. ________ God made woman from one of Adam's ribs.

f. ________ Adam expressed his appreciation for his wife.

Answer this question.

1.8 How do you know that God created language?

____

____

____

____

WORD STUDY

Certain words need to be identified by the way they are used in sentences. For example, you do not know how to pronounce the word *lead* until you see it used in a sentence. In the sentence, "I will lead the way," the *ea* has the long /ē/ sound. In the sentence, "The pencil was made of lead," the *ea* has the short /e/ sound. Words that are spelled the same but have different meanings and are pronounced differently are called *heteronyms.*

lead

lēad

re′ cord

re cord′

Heteronyms

Complete this activity.

1.9 Circle the respelling that tells how the word should be pronounced in the sentence.

a. The written *record* has provided a means through which people can remember history.
rek′ urd ri kôrd′

b. We *record* the events in order.
rek′ urd ri kôrd′

c. The *minute* you listen to a false report, you are in danger of hearing language abuse.
min′ it mī nüt′

d. The *minute* instructions helped me to do the work accurately.
min′ it mī nüt′

e. The *bow* broke when Fred pulled the string too hard.
bou bō

f. The performer took a *bow* and sang again.
bou bō

g. A man began to *wind* the grandfather clock.
wīnd wind

h. A strong *wind* carried the sailboat into the open sea.
wīnd wind

i. Jack *read* the book to his friend.
rēd red

j. Children should learn to *read* when they come to school.
rēd red

1.10 **Use the clues to complete the puzzle.**

A secret message needs to be unscrambled. Put it on the lines below the clues. Use the circled letters in the puzzle to decode the message. Some of the answers for the puzzle are included in the LIFEPAC vocabulary list.

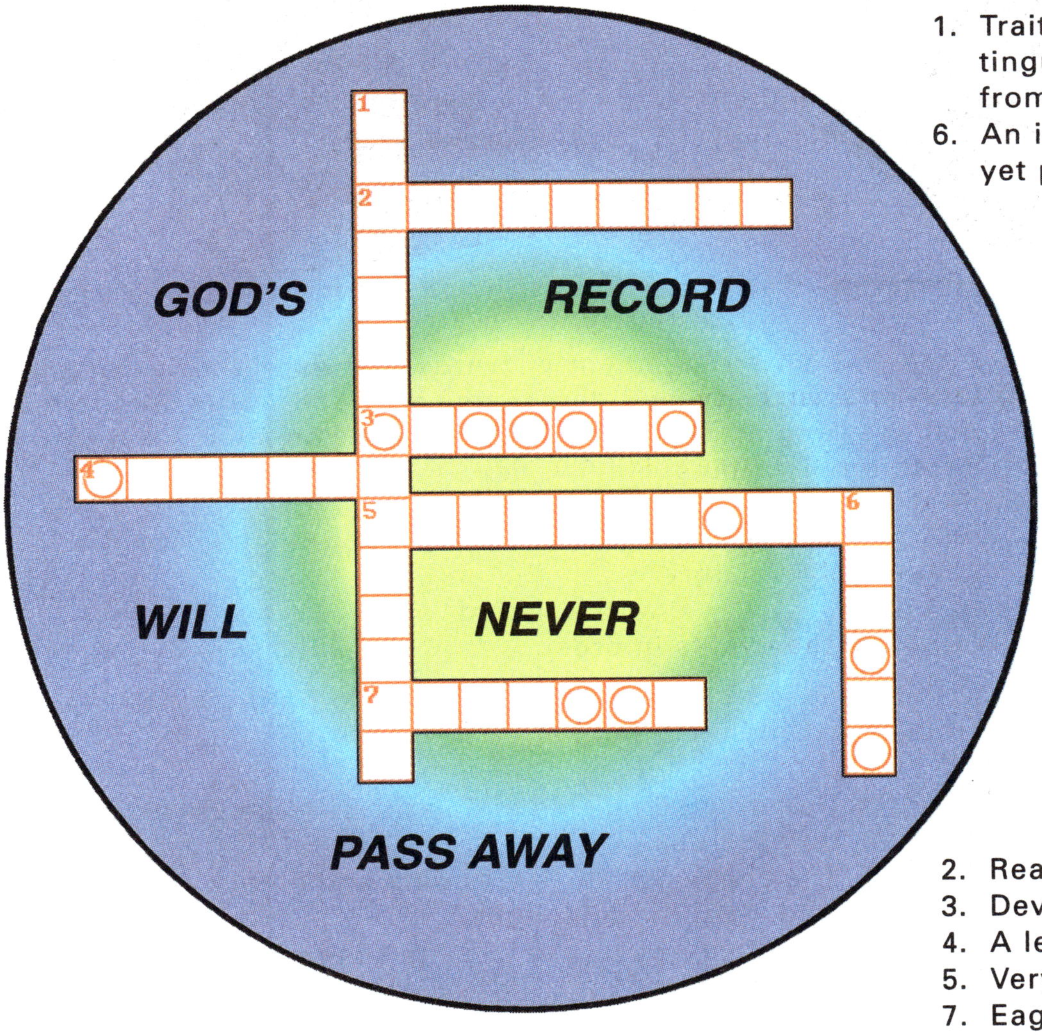

GOD'S RECORD WILL NEVER PASS AWAY

DOWN

1. Traits that distinguish people from each other.
6. An idea that is not yet proven.

ACROSS

2. Real
3. Developed gradually
4. A learned person
5. Very smart
7. Eager to know

SECRET MESSAGE: ____________ ____________ ____________.

Match each vocabulary word with its definition.

1.11	________	scholar	a. small unit of living matter
1.12	________	evolve	b. something that comes before something else
1.13	________	cell	c. a success in completing something
1.14	________	authentic	d. person having much knowledge after study
1.15	________	creation	e. recognizing a thing's worth
1.16	________	abuse	f. act of making something
1.17	________	harbinger	g. to unfold; develop gradually
1.18	________	unique	h. having no like or equal
1.19	________	accomplishment	i. helper; wife or husband
1.20	________	helpmeet	j. what it claims to be; real; genuine
1.21	________	appreciation	k. a test of knowledge
1.22	________	examination	l. use wrongly

COMPOSITION

A sentence is an arrangement of words that expresses a complete thought. A sentence can be written or spoken. If the words are in order, the person speaking or writing will communicate an idea to the person who is listening or reading.

Complete this activity.

1.23 Read the following word arrangements. Put an *S* on the line if the words produce a complete thought.

a. ______ God created heaven and earth with the power of His own words.

b. ______ The shapeless earth was dark and empty until God said, "Let there be light."

c. ______ Language reading is writing, speaking, and listening and.

d. ______ God communicated with the angels after He gave them the gift of language.

e. ______ Satan abused the gift of language, when he let his selfish pride control his thoughts.

f. ______ God is the originator of communication.

g. ______ God language when heaven earth used He created and.

h. ______ When we use the gift of language, we are reflecting God's image in us.

A group of words must be arranged into two parts to make a sentence. One part is the subject. The *subject* is a word or group of words about which something is said in a sentence. The other part of the sentence is the predicate. The *predicate* tells something about the subject. Example:

The blue book (subject) is the social studies book (predicate).

Complete this activity.

1.24 Divide the following sentences into their two parts. Circle the complete subject and draw a line under the complete predicate.

a. Missionaries in jungle territories work with native tribes.
b. God can talk.
c. John and his father played a game.
d. John planned to win the race.
e. Mother watched the children play.

HANDWRITING AND SPELLING

Handwriting and spelling are important skills. Proper use of both skills are necessary if other people are going to read what you write.

Handwriting. The capital letters in this lesson begin with a cane shape. Carefully study the manner in which each letter is formed.

N Z U V W X

Complete these handwriting activities.

1.25 Look at the examples and copy them on the following line.

1.26 Write each of the following words. Use a separate piece of handwriting paper.

Nebraska
Quebec
Utah
Vermont
Washington
Xenia

Teacher check ______________________________
Initial Date

Spelling. In an earlier LIFEPAC, you learned to spell words with vowel digraphs. We will continue with this same skill in words of many syllables. Follow the five-step spelling plan as you learn to spell the words from Spelling Words-1.

Spelling Words-1

automatic	jewelry	seventeenth
available	leadership	somersault
betrayal	maintenance	soothingly
exceedingly	meaningful	underneath
faithfully	neighborhood	uneasy
foolishness	newscaster	woodpecker
inauguration	remainder	

Complete these spelling activities.

1.27 Supply the missing vowel digraph for each of the following words.

a.	—tomatic	h.	j—elry	o.	sevent—nth
b.	av—lable	i.	l—dership	p.	somers—lt
c.	betr—al	j.	m—ntenance	q.	s—thingly
d.	exc—dingly	k.	m—ningful	r.	undern—th
e.	f—thfully	l.	neighborh—d	s.	un—sy
f.	f—lishness	m.	n—scaster	t.	w—dpecker
g.	in—guration	n.	rem—nder		

1.28 Group the spelling words according to vowel digraph sounds.

a. /au/ (as in *automobile*)

____

____

____

b. /ay/ (as in *pray*)

____

c. /ai/ (as in *rain*)

____

____

____

____

d. /oo/ (as in *good*)

____

____

e. /ew/ (as in *flew*)

____

____

f. /ee/ (as in *seed*)

____

____

g. /ea/ (as in *bean*)

____

____

____

____

h. /oo/ (as in *food*)

____

____

1.29 Write the number of vowel sounds you hear in each of the following words.

a. automatic ______

b. available ______

c. inauguration ______

d. maintenance ______

e. neighborhood ______

f. somersault ______

ABC ✓ **Ask your teacher to give you a practice spelling test of Spelling Words-1.** Restudy the words you missed.

Review the material in this section to prepare for the Self Test. The Self Test will check your understanding of this section. Any items you miss on this test will show you the areas you need to restudy.

SELF TEST 1

Write "S" on the line before each complete sentence (each item, 2 points).

1.01 ________ Adam and Eve in the garden.
1.02 ________ The serpent tempted Eve.
1.03 ________ Satan plotted against God.
1.04 ________ Agreement to leave heaven.
1.05 ________ God provided a Savior.
1.06 ________ Adam was given the gift of language.
1.07 ________ Created all the animals without giving them names.
1.08 ________ Adam felt lonely.
1.09 ________ God understood Adam's needs.
1.010 ________ Man talking to another person.

Put the following events in the correct order (each event, 3 points).

1.011 ________ Adam named the animals.
1.012 ________ God created the animals.
1.013 ________ God created woman.
1.014 ________ God brought the animals to Adam.
1.015 ________ God knew Adam should have a companion.

Draw one line under each subject and two lines under each predicate (each sentence, 3 points).

1.016 People the world over need salvation.

1.017 Bill and his friends attend church.

1.018 God sent His only begotten Son.

Underline the correct pronunciation for each heteronym (each answer, 3 points).

1.019 Please wind the clock before coming to bed.

wind wīnd

1.020 He sat in the bow of the boat.

bou bō

Answer the questions about the following paragraph (each answer, 4 points).

People can create words by performing a famous deed. An example of a famous deed creating a word is the word *pasteurize.* The word means the process of heating raw milk to kill germs. This process was discovered by Louis Pasteur. All milk that is safe to drink has been *pasteurized.* Mr. Pasteur invented a safe way to prepare milk and, in the process, invented a new word.

1.021 What new word was invented? ______________________

1.022 Who invented a new process? ______________________

1.023 How are the germs killed? ______________________

1.024 What kind of milk must be pasteurized? ______________________

1.025 What is one way new words are added to our language? ________
____

1.026 When is milk safe to drink? ______________________
____

Write the main idea for the paragraph (this answer, 5 points).

1.027 ____
____

Write a definition for each word (each definition, 4 points).

1.028 creation ______________________________________

1.029 helpmeet ______________________________________

1.030 harbinger ______________________________________

1.031 unique ______________________________________

Answer this question. Use a complete sentence. (this answer, 5 points).

1.032 When and where did man first use language?

____
____

Possible Score	100
My Score	______
Teacher check	______________ Initial Date

Take your spelling test of Spelling Words-1.

II. SECTION TWO

In this section, you will learn several ways in which our language is abused. You will practice skills that will help you improve your reading and writing. You will learn how to make a time line, and you will work with some very special types of words and meanings.

Review these objectives. When you have completed this section, you should be able to:

6. Define new words.
9. Write the capital letters *N* through *Z* in cursive handwriting.
10. Spell new words.
11. Identify cause and effect statements in written material.
12. Identify propaganda techniques in advertisements.
13. Write a short summary of what you have read.
14. Change the meaning of root words by adding prefixes.
15. Identify and use adjectives and adverbs.

Restudy these vocabulary words.

confession	opportunity	subtle
disobedience	sacrifice	unacceptable

ABUSED LANGUAGE IN THE GARDEN

Remember Lucifer? "How did he get back in the picture?" you might ask. The story is very sad, but is necessary to understand the growth and development of language.

God had cast Lucifer out of heaven when Lucifer's pride had become so great that he wanted to overthrow God and become like God. Lucifer became known as Satan. It is hard for us to understand why God allowed Satan to influence His most prized creation, but God did allow Satan to tempt man.

Let's learn about a conversation between Eve and Satan. This conversation took place in the garden and is recorded in Genesis chapter 3. In this passage of Scripture, Satan is referred to as "the serpent." (He is also referred to as the serpent in Revelation 12:9, 14, and 15.) He probably received this title because of his subtle ways of deceiving people.

Perhaps Eve had seen Satan before their conversation. She had no reason to fear or to avoid him. He was a beautiful creature, and God allowed him to be in the garden. Perhaps she listened willingly to Satan because "...Satan himself is transformed into an angel of light" (2 Corinthians 11:14).

When Satan spoke, he abused the language of mankind. Satan, the serpent, asked a question which planted doubt in Eve's thoughts. This question is the first record we have of twisting the meaning of words in order to make them deceive the listener.

Read Genesis chapter 3. The serpent asked Eve the question, "...hath God said, Ye shall not eat of every tree of the garden?"

Eve answered, "We may eat of the fruit of the trees of the garden: but of the fruit of the tree which is in the midst of the garden, God hath said, Ye shall not eat of it...lest ye die."

The serpent then planted doubt about God's honesty in Eve's mind with these words (Genesis 3:4, 5), "...Ye shall not surely die: For God doth know that in the day ye eat thereof, then your eyes shall be opened, and ye shall be as gods, knowing good and evil." The serpent used that language to make it appear that God was not honest and was trying to keep Adam and Eve from becoming all they could be!

Eve believed the serpent and looked at the fruit on the forbidden tree. It looked delicious, so she touched it, ate it, and shared it with Adam. Adam and Eve were very different from that time on. Read Genesis 3:7–24 to find out what happened to them and to the serpent after they ate the forbidden fruit.

Cause and effect. The word *cause* refers to the person, thing, or event that made something happen. When we want to know why something happened, we look for the *cause*.

Many people want to know why Adam and Eve sinned. The *cause* was that they listened to Satan and said, "Yes," when Satan tempted them.

The word *effect* refers to the *result* of the cause. For every effect or result, there is also a cause. The *effect* is *that which was made to happen by a person, thing, or event.*

Many authors use cause and effect to build the plot of a story. Sometimes writers give the effect first and keep the reader guessing about the cause until near the end of the story. The ability to read a story and find the cause and effect is an important skill to develop.

Complete this activity.

2.1 Read the following sentences. Draw one line under each cause and two lines under each effect.

a. Johnny was anxious to get to school on time. He rode his bicycle through his neighbor's flower garden.
b. "Johnny!" screamed the angry neighbor, "You are destroying the beautiful flowers!"
c. Lucifer decided to become greater than Jehovah God. God cast him out of heaven.
d. The children in the neighborhood teased Mickey every day. Mickey ran home crying.

Cause and Effect

Propaganda. We have seen one way in which Satan abused our language. People, too, abuse our language in various ways. One way with which you are probably most familiar is the propaganda that is found in different advertising. Because this form of propaganda will continue to be widely used, you should learn to recognize it.

Propaganda

Propaganda is the spreading of opinions or beliefs. These opinions or beliefs may be supported by facts or they may not be supported by facts. Not all advertising claims are false. Honest business owners realize that having a good product and being honest with customers will improve business. However, much advertising is only an opinion of the people attempting to sell the product. The intelligent buyer will sort the truth from the untruth.

Complete this activity.

Use this list of advertising techniques:

2.2 1. "Our product is better than all other products."

2. "You need this product in order to have everything your neighbors have."

3. "Our product is not as expensive as other products."

4. "Our product will keep your family healthy and free from danger."

Read each line from the following advertisements. Decide which technique is being used to try to sell you a product. Write the number 1, 2, 3, or 4 on the line according to the technique you choose.

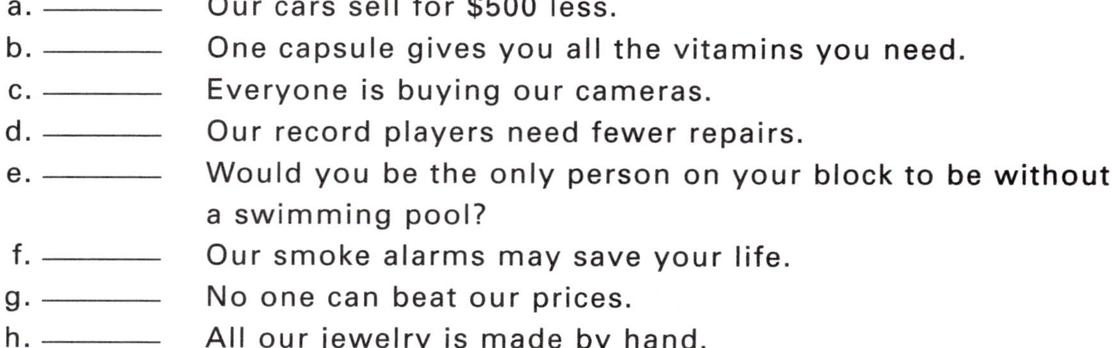

a. ______ Our cars sell for $500 less.

b. ______ One capsule gives you all the vitamins you need.

c. ______ Everyone is buying our cameras.

d. ______ Our record players need fewer repairs.

e. ______ Would you be the only person on your block to be without a swimming pool?

f. ______ Our smoke alarms may save your life.

g. ______ No one can beat our prices.

h. ______ All our jewelry is made by hand.

A FATAL ARGUMENT AND A FLAT DENIAL

When Adam and Eve listened to Satan and ate fruit from the Tree of the Knowledge of Good and Evil, they were guilty of the sin of **disobedience**. Adam and Eve immediately became sinners. Sin changed them and God had to take them out of the beautiful garden so that they would not eat of the tree of life.

Adam and Eve were given two sons, Cain and Abel. These boys were taught how to worship God. Cain became a farmer, and Abel raised sheep. Both men had learned the rules for bringing a **sacrifice** to God. Abel chose to offer the best of his flock because that offering was pleasing to God. Cain chose to bring his best fruit. This offering was **unacceptable** to God because it was not an animal offering. Animal offerings were a symbol of man's **confession** of sin and his need for a Savior. They also reminded man that the wages of sin is death.

Cain became very jealous of his brother when he saw that God had accepted Abel's offering. God spoke to Cain about his attitude, but Cain did not ask God to forgive him. Instead of asking God's forgiveness for not bringing a blood sacrifice, Cain talked it over with Abel. They were unable to settle their differences, and Cain killed his brother. Jealousy and a bad attitude can lead to sinful thoughts and an abuse of language in our conversations. It also can lead to terrible actions.

God gave Cain another **opportunity** to confess his sin. God asked Cain a question. Do you remember the question God asked Adam? God knew what Cain had done, but He wanted him to confess. God wants us always to confess if we have done a wrong thing. Questions help us think about what we have done. When God asked Cain where his brother Abel was, Cain lied. *Lying is an abuse of the gift of language.* Denying our wrongdoing keeps us from God's forgiveness. Denying our wrong pleases God's enemy, Satan. Genesis 4:1–6 tells the story of

Cain's discussions with his brother and God. When you read the story, you will understand how a person's words tell what kind of attitude he has.

A *summary* is a short statement about what you have read. When you write a summary, you should use the following steps:

1 Identify the main idea.
2. Recall the *important* details that tell about the main idea.
3. Write the main idea and the important details in complete sentences.

This process is like making an outline of what you have read, except that you divide your summary into paragraphs and you always use complete sentences.

A summary of the last paragraph of the story about Cain and Abel would look like this:

God gave Cain a chance to confess his sin. God wanted Cain to confess, but Cain lied. This lie kept Cain from being forgiven.

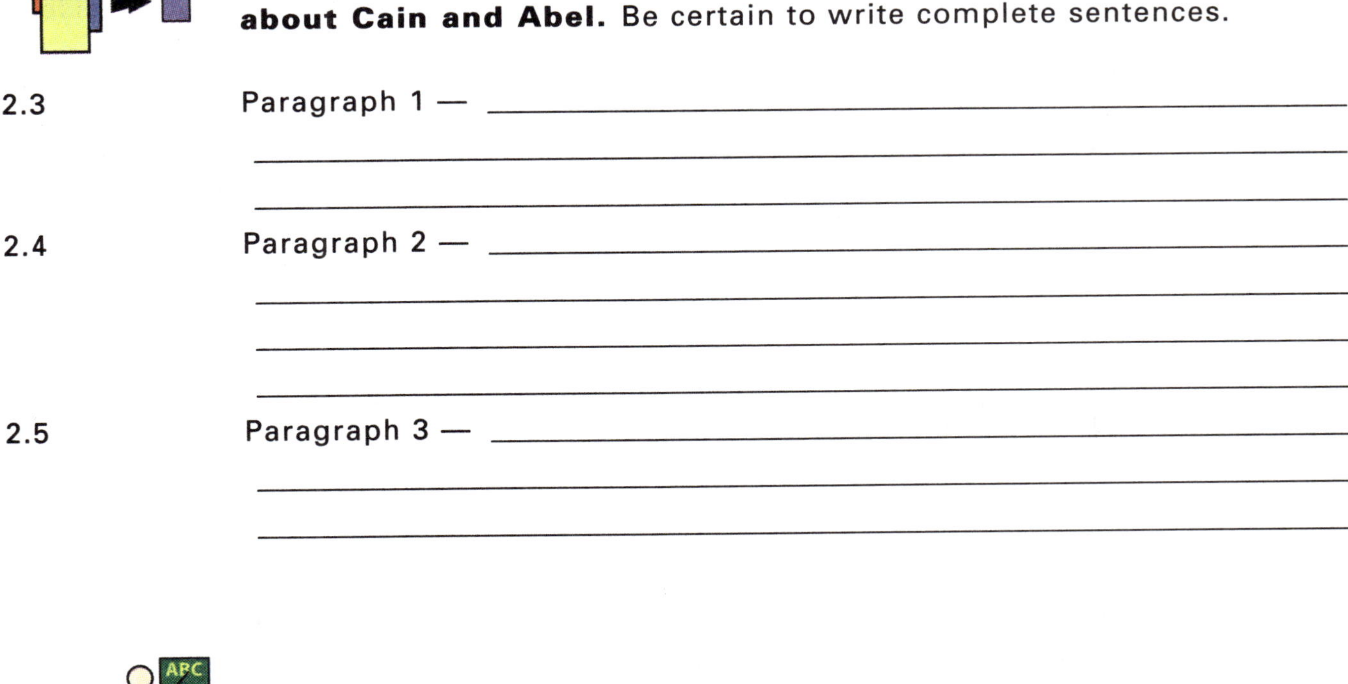

Write a summary of the first three paragraphs of the story about Cain and Abel. Be certain to write complete sentences.

2.3 Paragraph 1 — ______________________________

____

____

2.4 Paragraph 2 — ______________________________

____

____

____

2.5 Paragraph 3 — ______________________________

____

____

Teacher check ______________________________

Initial Date

PREFIXES AND SUFFIXES

The meaning of a word can be changed by adding a letter, or a set of letters, to the root word. If the addition is placed at the beginning of the root word, it is called a *prefix*. If the letters or sets of letters are placed at the end of a word, it is called a *suffix*. Some words have both a prefix and a suffix added to the root word. Prefixes and suffixes are also referred to as *affixes* because they are "stuck on", or affixed, to the root word.

Complete this activity.

2.6 Classify each affix below as a prefix or a suffix, and write the root word on the line. For instance, if a prefix has been added to a root word, place an X in the prefix column. If a suffix has been added, mark the suffix column. Mark both columns if both a prefix and suffix have been added.

		Prefix	**Suffix**	**Root Word**
a.	Germanic	______	______	__________
b.	approximately	______	______	__________
c.	translation	______	______	__________
d.	factual	______	______	__________
e.	uneventful	______	______	__________
f.	unappreciative	______	______	__________
g.	nomadic	______	______	__________
h.	unintelligently	______	______	__________
i.	disobeyed	______	______	__________
j.	impatient	______	______	__________
k.	disadvantage	______	______	__________
l.	inaccurate	______	______	__________
m.	misinterpret	______	______	__________

A prefix can change the meaning of a word. One meaning for the prefixes *un-*, *im-*, and *in-* is "not." If the prefix *un-* is added to the root word *happy*, the word **un***happy* is formed. **Un***happy* means *not happy.*

Complete this activity.

2.7 Add the appropriate prefix *un-*, *im-*, or *in-* to the root word to change the meaning.

a.	______	intelligent	f.	______	skilled
b.	______	expensive	g.	______	mature
c.	______	patient	h.	______	perfect
d.	______	accurate	i.	______	popular
e.	______	correct	j.	______	common

Other prefixes can also change the meaning of root words. Study the following prefixes to determine how they add to or change the meaning of the root word.

Prefix Definition	Prefix		Root Word		New Word
against	anti-	+	social	=	antisocial
not	dis-	+	please	=	displease
two	bi-	+	cycle	=	bicycle
wrong	mis-	+	lead	=	mislead
not	non-	+	fiction	=	nonfiction
before	pre-	+	arrange	=	prearrange
in favor of	pro-	+	American	=	pro-American
again	re-	+	place	=	replace
over or above	super-	+	natural	=	supernatural

Complete each statement. Write the words made with prefixes from the preceding list.

2.8 Four boys rode in the ________________ race.

2.9 Speaking to your neighbor in a friendly way is not ________________ .

2.10 Father and Mother told Bobby about the way man began to ________________ God.

2.11 A story that tells the facts is ________________ .

2.12 The teacher made an effort to ________________ a visit with the mayor.

2.13 Those ______________________ travelers saluted the flag daily.

2.14 To ______________________ an antique table is usually impossible.

2.15 God's creative acts are ______________________ .

2.16 One who tells the truth does not ______________________ the people.

Suffixes can add to the meanings of root words. Adding the suffix *-ful* to the word *cheer* produces the word *cheerful*, which means *full of cheer*. Adding the suffix *-less* to the word *home* produces the word *homeless*, which means *without a home*. Adding the suffix *-able* to the word *read* produces the word *readable*, which means *able to be read*. Many other suffixes add to the meanings of root words in the same way.

Add suffixes to the following root words. Choose either *-ful, -less,* or *-able* to fit the given definition.

2.17

a.	print	____________	able to be printed
b.	truth	____________	full of truth
c.	use	____________	without use
d.	hope	____________	full of hope
e.	move	____________	able to be moved
f.	change	____________	able to be changed
g.	joy	____________	full of joy
h.	end	____________	without end
i.	trust	____________	full of trust
j.	sleep	____________	without sleep

A suffix can also change a word in the following ways:

A word can become a *noun* by adding a suffix. A noun is a word that names a person, place, or thing.

A word can become an *adjective* by adding a suffix. An adjective is a word that describes a noun.

A word can become an *adverb* by adding a suffix. An adverb is a word that describes a verb.

Suffixes can change the number of a thing or the time of an action.

LANGUAGE ARTS 503

LIFEPAC TEST

80
100

Name ______________________

Date ______________________

Score ______________________

LANGUAGE ARTS 503
LIFEPAC TEST

Answer *true* **or** *false* (each answer, 1 point).

1. ______________ The main idea of a selection is usually found in the first or last sentence.
2. ______________ Details are a very unimportant part of reading.
3. ______________ Propaganda is found only in newspaper advertisements.
4. ______________ An author usually has a definite purpose for writing something.
5. ______________ A time line can be used to picture events in history.
6. ______________ Details support the main idea of a selection.
7. ______________ Trying to influence you to "keep up with your neighbors" is one propaganda technique used in advertising.
8. ______________ The Bible was written to entertain.
9. ______________ A summary is somewhat like an outline.
10. ______________ A summary should include as much information as possible.

Put the events from Genesis chapter 3 in order (each event, 3 points).

11. ________ The serpent plants doubt in Eve's mind.
12. ________ Eve gave some fruit to Adam.
13. ________ Eve believes the serpent.
14. ________ The serpent questions Eve.
15. ________ Eve ate the fruit.

Circle the correct pronunciation for each heteronym (each answer, 3 points).

16. Where did you *record* the information?
rek′ urd ri kôrd′

17. Can you work with *minute* details?
min′ it mī nüt′

Write an "S" **on the line in front of each complete sentence** (each item, 2 points).

18. ________ Driven from the garden by God.
19. ________ Adam and Eve sinned.
20. ________ God will forgive us our sins.

Draw one line under the subject and two lines under each predicate (each sentence, 3 points).

21. The Bible record proves that God used language.
22. The power and ability to communicate is a divine characteristic.

Draw one line under each cause and two lines under each effect (each sentence, 3 points).

23. The boy was injured when he fell from his bicycle.
24. Due to carelessness, the car was not repaired correctly.
25. The ice melted when we forgot to put it in the freezer.

Add a prefix or suffix to each root word to change or add to its meaning (each answer, 3 points).

26. care ________
27. ________visible
28. ________desirable
29. agree ________
30. ________patient

Draw one line under each adjective and two lines under each adverb (each sentence, 2 points).

31. The enormous truck ran wildly out of control.
32. Sailing swiftly with the breeze the sleek sailboat set a record.
33. A refreshing nap is often enjoyed after work.

Match the homonyms with their meaning (each answer, 2 points).

34. ________ site — a. a place to make sacrifices
35. ________ cite — b. to quote
36. ________ altar — c. to change
37. ________ alter — d. a place on which to build

Write a definition for each idiom (each definition, 5 points).

38. My neighbor *gave me a lift* into town because it was too far to walk.

____

39. The old man *spun a yarn* that was hard to believe.

____

Answer this question (this answer, 5 points).

40. How did man begin to use language?

____

____

Name the type of propaganda technique used in this statement (this answer, 4 points).

41. Our cereal builds strong bodies.

____

Take your LIFEPAC Spelling Test.

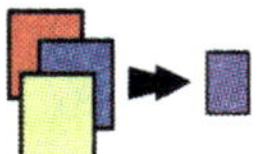

Study the following root words and the new words made by adding suffixes. Use the new words to complete the sentences.

Root Word		Suffix		New Word		Kind of Word
kind	+	-ly	=	kindly	=	adverb
sweet	+	-en	=	sweeten	=	verb
write	+	-er	=	writer	=	noun
allow	+	-ance	=	allowance	=	noun
pain	+	-less	=	painless	=	adjective
sing	+	-ing	=	singing	=	verb
please	+	-ant	=	pleasant	=	adjective
laugh	+	-ed	=	laughed	=	verb

2.18 The a. ____________ woman spoke b. ____________ to the grouchy paper boy.

2.19 Father had to ____________ the coffee with sugar.

2.20 The monk was a ____________ of early manuscripts.

2.21 Children ____________ at the silly animal clown.

2.22 A food ____________ is needed to keep the body healthy.

2.23 The doctor tried to treat the wound in a ____________ way.

2.24 ____________ was a favorite pastime of the man who wrote the Twenty-Third Psalm.

Write a definition for each of the following vocabulary words.

2.25 abuse ____________

2.26 confession ____________

2.27 disobedience ____________

2.28 opportunity ____________

2.29 sacrifice ____________

2.30 scholar ____________

2.31 subtle ____________

2.32 unacceptable ____________

COMPOSITION

Phrases. Putting words together to make a meaningful sentence is done phrase by phrase. Phrases are groups of words within a sentence. Phrases give meaningful information to the reader of a sentence, such as: who, what, which, when, where, why, and how.

Match the phrases to form a sentence. Study the phrases in columns A, B, and C. Match the phrases and write the sentences on the numbered lines. **Use a phrase from each column.**

A	B	C
The little bird	found	the lost boys.
Strong boys	learned to farm	flower seeds.
Early people	can fly	to the moon.
Astronauts	can run	the land.
The friendly dog	learned to eat	a mile.

2.33 ______________________________

2.34 ______________________________

2.35 ______________________________

2.36 ______________________________

2.37 ______________________________

Adjectives. Adjectives are words that describe nouns or pronouns. Adjectives help you form pictures in your mind. These pictures make reading and listening more interesting. They help make learning easier and more enjoyable. Adjectives tell ***what kind, how many, which***, or ***whose*** about a noun or a pronoun.

Note: Adjectives such as ***the, a, an, this, these***, and ***all*** can place limits on nouns. Possessive forms of nouns (*his, her, Susan's*) and numbers and expressions of quantity (*gallon, ton, third*) are also adjectives.

Complete these activities.

2.38 Draw a line under each adjective in each of the following sentences.

a. A beautiful butterfly flew around the yard.

b. The thoughtful teacher helped us with our homework.

c. The fussy children refused to eat their carrots.

d. We saw a sparkling diamond displayed in the window.

e. The class was for serious students.

2.39 Choose an adjective from the following list to complete each sentence.

enormous	prosperous
adventurous	moonlit
unbearable	memorable

a. The ____________________ man gave away large sums of money.
b. We can see well on a ____________________ night.
c. The ____________________ heat forced the workers inside.
d. The signing of the Declaration of Independence was a ____________________ event.
e. The ____________________ group backpacked into the wilderness.
f. We could not see the tops of the ____________________ trees.

Adverbs. Adverbs modify verbs, adjectives, or other adverbs. They tell how, where, when, or to what extent. These words help us understand what is happening in a sentence. Adverbs are often formed by adding the suffix *-ly* to an adjective.

Complete these activities.

2.40 Underline the adverbs in each of the following sentences.

a. Mary and Tom work well together.
b. We go to the store often.
c. Bob whistled loudly as he walked home.
d. The snake crawled slowly through the grass.
e. The ship sailed smoothly across the bay.
f. My uncle was a very great storyteller.

2.41 Write a sentence using the adverb listed in front of each line.

a. often ____________________
b. very ____________________
c. well ____________________
d. carefully ____________________
e. boldly ____________________

Teacher check ____________________
Initial Date

HANDWRITING AND SPELLING

Practice your handwriting and spelling skills daily. You should apply these skills to all your writing assignments.

Handwriting. The capital letters *Y* and *Z* begin with a cane shape and go below the baseline. They and J are the only capital letters that go below the baseline. Carefully study how they are formed.

Y Z Y Z Y Z J

Complete these handwriting activities.

2.42 Look at the examples and copy them on the following line.

2.43 Write each of the following words. Use a separate piece of handwriting paper.

Yugoslavia	Zambesi
Yukon	Zion
Yuma	Zurich

Spelling. Spelling a word is easy when you can hear all the sounds that the letters represent. Many words contain silent letters, which make spelling them much more difficult. In this spelling lesson, you will look for the silent letters. Continue to use the five-step spelling plan as you learn to spell the words from Spelling Words-2.

Spelling Words-2

bristle	folks	knight	stalk
chalk	freight	knot	wreckage
daughter	glisten	knowledge	wrench
fasten	hasten	salmon	wrestle
flight	kneel	sigh	wrist

Complete these spelling activities.

2.44 Write each spelling word in your best handwriting.

a. ____________________
b. ____________________
c. ____________________
d. ____________________
e. ____________________
f. ____________________
g. ____________________
h. ____________________
i. ____________________
j. ____________________
k. ____________________
l. ____________________
m. ____________________
n. ____________________
o. ____________________
p. ____________________
q. ____________________
r. ____________________
s. ____________________
t. ____________________

Teacher check ______________________________
Initial Date

2.45 Write the missing silent letters on the lines.

a. bris__le
b. __neel
c. __ni__t
d. __rist
e. cha__k
f. has__en
g. __nowledge
h. __res__le
i. dau__ter
j. glis__en
k. __rench
l. fas__en
m. frei__t
n. __not
o. __reckage
p. sa__mon
q. fo__ks
r. si__
s. fli__t
t. sta__k

2.46 Group the spelling words according to their silent letters. Some words will be used more than once.

a. **silent "t"**	b. **silent "k"**	c. **silent "w"**
______________	______________	______________
______________	______________	______________
______________	______________	______________
______________	______________	______________
______________	______________	______________
______________	______________	______________

d. **silent "l"**

____

____

____

____

____

e. **silent "gh"**

____

____

____

____

____

2.47 Unscramble the following words.

a. ceagwerk ______________
b. mnosla ______________
c. stenigl ______________
d. ghnikt ______________
e. sterlew ______________

2.48 Write a sentence using each of the following spelling words.

a. bristle ______________
b. fasten ______________
c. glisten ______________
d. hasten ______________
e. knowledge ______________
f. sigh ______________
g. stalk ______________
h. wreckage ______________
i. wrench ______________
j. wrist ______________

Ask your teacher to give you a practice spelling test of Spelling Words-2. Restudy the words you missed.

Review the material in this section to prepare for the Self Test. The Self Test will check your understanding of this section and will review the first section. Any items you miss on this test will show you the areas you need to restudy.

SELF TEST 2

Draw one line under each adjective and two lines under each adverb (each sentence, 2 points).

2.01 The disgusted player walked slowly back to the dugout.

2.02 We often ride the elevator to the top of the towering skyscraper.

2.03 The modest woman meekly accepted the award.

2.04 The work was efficiently completed by the intelligent students.

2.05 That ancient vehicle is not running well.

Write an "S" on the blank in front of each complete sentence (each item, 2 points).

2.06 ________ Cain was very jealous of Abel.

2.07 ________ Offering very pleasing to God.

2.08 ________ Denying our sins and keeping us from God.

2.09 ________ God gave Cain a chance to confess.

2.010 ________ God accepted Abel's offering.

Draw one line under each complete subject and two lines under each complete predicate (each sentence, 3 points).

2.011 The boy in the back seat was jumping up and down.

2.012 Everyone in town went to the parade.

2.013 We had fun at the zoo.

2.014 Our radio and our record player are not working.

2.015 Have you studied for the test?

Add a prefix to each root word to change the meaning (each answer, 3 points).

2.016 ________ safe

2.017 ________ correct

2.018 ________ proper

2.019 ________ human

2.020 ________ even

Add a suffix to each root word to change the meaning (each answer, 3 points).

2.021 home ________

2.022 cheer ________

2.023 truth ________

2.024 print ________

2.025 sleep ________

Draw one line under the cause and two under the effect (each sentence, 3 points).

2.026 Adam and Eve became sinners when they ate from the tree of the knowledge of good and evil.

2.027 Cain became very jealous when he saw that God accepted Abel's offering.

2.028 Denying our sins keeps us from God's forgiveness.

2.029 Lucifer wanted to overthrow God, so he was cast out of heaven.

2.030 Cain was not forgiven of his sin because he refused to ask God to forgive him.

Name the type of propaganda technique used in each statement (each answer, 5 points).

2.031 Our cereal builds strong bodies.

____

2.032 Our cars give you years of dependable service.

____

2.033 Buy this car now while it can be sold at bargain prices.

____

2.034 Who wants to be the only overweight person at the party?
Buy CONTROL to help you diet.

____

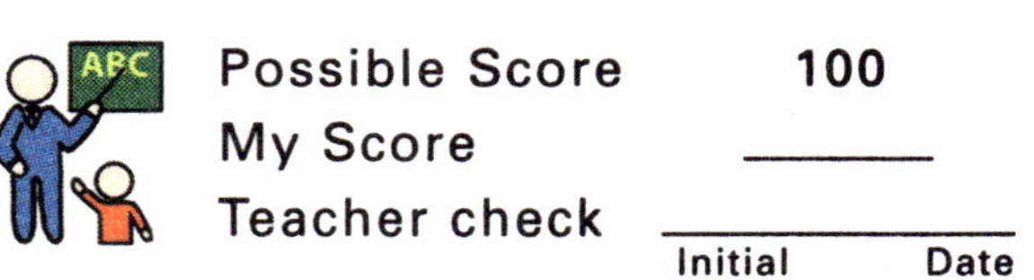

Take your spelling test of Spelling Words-2.

III. SECTION THREE

For many years after God took Adam and Eve out of the garden, mankind used one language. Sin had entered the thoughts of everyone, and people had wicked thoughts and actions. God finally washed the whole earth with a great flood. Only one family of people and two of each kind of animal were saved.

The human survivors of the Flood and their descendants spoke one language. The people of Shinar were proud of themselves and wanted to be remembered forever and ever. They were eager to make a name for themselves.

These Shinar people were skilled builders. They knew how to make bricks that would last for centuries. They had great pride in their accomplishments. Their pride led them to plan a skyscraper at Babel that would reach to heaven. These people thought their skyscraper would make a name for them that everyone would respect, as well as provide protection for them.

God inspected the work these people had accomplished. He looked at the city and the tower. It was magnificent! Wasn't man creative? As God observed man's creative efforts, He read their thoughts. The magnificence and the creativity were good, but the pride behind the plan was wrong. God immediately made a change in the Shinar people that forced a change in their plans. God said, "...let us go down, and there confound their language, that they may not understand one another's speech."(Genesis 11:7)

Imagine what great confusion that caused! People from that time on spoke many different languages. This process of change began when God confused the language of the people in Shinar. The plan to build the tower to heaven could not be carried out.

Because people spoke differently from each other, the building of the tower soon stopped. People began to scatter all over the earth. The story of the languages of the world began with the tower of Babel.

Review these objectives. When you have completed this section, you should be able to:

6. Define new words.
9. Write the capital letters *N* through *Z* in cursive handwriting.
10. Spell new words.
16. Identify an author's purpose.
17. Develop a historical time line.
18. Write definitions for homonyms.
19. Express the literal meaning of idioms.
20. Write a descriptive short story.

Restudy these vocabulary words.

abound	Germanic	revenge
cobbler	gourmet	scop
entangle	monk	squire
environment	nomadic	

AUTHOR'S PURPOSE

You must develop many important comprehension skills in order to become a good reader. Many of these skills you have already studied in this LIFEPAC. These comprehension skills include learning to find the main idea and learning to put events in sequence.

Another important skill is learning to determine why an author wrote a particular article, story, or book. The author may want to entertain you, to inform you of something, to give you certain facts, to give you a set of directions, or to influence your thinking. As you are reading, you should think about why the author is writing. Finding the author's purpose will help you understand and enjoy what you are reading.

Read the following article and story so that you can answer questions about the author's purpose.

The Anglo-Saxon language. The history of language is very exciting. It is fascinating to read about the building of the Tower of Babel, the Bible story that explains why people scattered all over the earth, were speaking different languages. We accept this explanation because we believe the Bible contains factual information and can be accepted as truth.

Sometime during the nineteenth century (1800s), scholars began tracing the history of the English language. By comparing English root words that expressed the same ideas as Greek, Latin, and German root words, they discovered similarities.

In the search for the history of language, the scholars learned that in very, very early times, people were **nomadic**. Their travels from place to place to get food eventually led them from Asia into parts of Europe. Small groups settled in different places and each group developed its own language. This information is supported by the record given in the Bible. The English language came from **Germanic** people. They were Germanic because they originated in the region known as Germany and spread throughout Europe. Approximately fifteen hundred years ago, Germanic people living in Central Europe, known as the Angles, moved to England. They were joined there by another Germanic tribe known as Saxons. Each tribe had its own language. When the two tribes settled down together, the two languages soon mixed. A new language was born, known as Anglo-Saxon, or Old English.

The oldest epic poem written in English is **Beowulf**. It may have been composed as early as the eighth century A.D. (700s) and was written down later in Old English. The heroic story itself takes place in an earlier time in Northern Europe—what is now Denmark and Sweden. It concerns two Germanic tribes that eventually spilled over the sea into

England: the Danes and the Geats. These were the Anglo–Saxon's ancestors, and the long poem describes the feats of the greatest hero of the time – Beowulf.

The story of Beowulf. The story begins when the king of the Danes, King Hrothgar (roth' gär) builds a great feasting hall named Heorot (hē' u rōt), which means hart or deer. In fact, mounted above the entrance to the hall is a large set of antlers. King Hrothgar is a good king, so the people often meet in the "horned house" to feast, fellowship, and listen to stories of the old heroes, set to harp music and told by the **scops**. But Grendel (gren'dul) the monster, half man and half beast, lives nearby in a muddy lake that is surrounded by swampland. Grendel despises sounds of mirth (joy, laughter) that come from the hall each night. Therefore, every night Grendel comes to Heorot and kills as many of Kings Hrothgar's people as he can. King Hrothgar and his thares (warriors) try to fight, but they are helpless because Grendel is magically protected: swords bounce harmlessly off his skin! The people live in terror.

Twelve winters pass. The walker in the darkness continues to maim the Danes, returning to the swamps at day break. The hoary (gray-or white-haired) old King Hrothgar loses all hope. Heorot stands empty and joyless. Harps are no longer heard.

One day, Beowulf (bā' ō wu̇lf) arrives with fourteen thanes from Geatland (Sweden). From across the whale-road (sea), he has heard about King Hrothgar's terrible situation. Beowulf is thane to King Hygelac (hī' gu lak) of the Geats and has a reputation for heroic deeds. He offers to fight Grendel for King Hrothgar and kill him if he can. King Hrothgar gladly accepts, noticing that Beowulf is big, strong, and carries himself with confidence. He holds a **gourmet** feast and Heorot is once again filled with merriment and singing. Everyone hopes that Beowulf can rid the land of the evil Grendel.

One of King Hrothgar's advisers, Unferth scofs at Beowulf's bravery, pointing out that Beowulf's great sword Naegling (nā' gling) cannot hurt Gendel. Beowulf responds by laying aside his weapons; he will fight Grendel with his bare hands! Soon the feasting is over and the Danes leave Heorot. Only Beowulf and his comitatus (cämu' tä dus; band of loyal followers) are left to wait for Grendel's coming.

Late into the night, all but Beowulf have fallen asleep inside Heorot, waiting for the monster. All fires have burned out and it is extremely dark. Beowulf's eyelids are heavy and he is almost asleep when he suddenly smells the odor of the moors (boggy swamps). Without further warning, Grendel crashes into the hall, pounces on the nearest sleeping warrior, and wreaks havoc. Beowulf springs to his feet and grabs one of Grendel's wrists, seizing it with an iron grip. Grendel screams in pain and fear. He thrashes about madly, doing great damage to the hall, but cannot get free of Beowulf. The two are **entangled** in a fierce struggle. Eventually, Grendel's struggles are so desperate and Beowulf's steely grip so powerful that the monster's arm separates from his body and comes off at the shoulder, leaving Beowulf holding a hairy arm with a now useless claw at the end. Grendel flees back through the fen–slopes to the lake, mortally wounded. The Danes are once again free from terror!

The next day, a grateful King Hrothgar throws an even bigger feast. Everyone praises Beowulf's courage, cunning, and strength. Even Unferth admits that Beowulf has performed heroically. The king and queen give Beowulf many gifts, including a powerful helmet to protect his head and a strong mail–shirt (an armored shirt made of metal links called chain mail). There is much rejoicing and singing and everyone lays down to sleep in the hall that night, free from the fear of attack.

The next morning they awake to discover that King Hrothgar's closest friend has been snatched away during the night and killed by Grendel's Mother in revenge for the loss of her son. The seahag lives at the bottom of the murky mere (lake), where she has returned to plan further evil for the Danes. Beowulf promises the mournful king that he will pursue Grendel's Mother and exact justice.

Beowulf and his band of shield bearers travel through the misty moor to the edge of the lake. He orders his men to stay behind, he will go in alone. He prepares by putting on his brand new helmet and mail—shirt. Unferth, who has come along, offers Beowulf the use of his sword Hrunting. Beowulf accepts it and plunges into the depths of the dark, icy water.

Large tentacles immediately grab him and draw him into a dry, underwater den. The tentacles belong to Grendel's Mother, who squeezes Beowulf with brute strength, hoping to crush the life out of him. But the helmet and chain mail are stronger and they withstand the crushing. Beowulf wrestles free and attacks the she-monster with Hrunting, but as with Grendel it merely bounces off her scaly skin. Beowulf remains calm and tries to think of another way to beat the seahag. He spies a great magical sword that was made by giants hanging on the wall of the cave. He grabs it with both hands and swings with all his might. The sword cuts right through the monster, killing her. Her blood is a powerful poison acid, and it melts the blade of the sword. Beowulf emerges triumphantly from the lake carrying the jeweled hilt of the giants' sword.

There is more celebration and feasting before Beowulf sails back over the have-way to his home. Later, Beowulf becomes king and fights and outwits a deadly dragon. But you can read about that on your own. There are several versions of Beowulf written for young readers. Check them out at your library. You will see that Beowulf is one of the earliest and most courageous of heroes.

Underline the correct answer for each question.

3.1 Why was the article about the Angles and Saxons written?
to entertain
to inform
to give directions

3.2 Why was the story of Beowulf written?
to entertain
to inform
to give directions

Answer these questions about why certain materials are written.

3.3 Why are cookbooks written? ______________________
3.4 Why are most novels written? ______________________
3.5 Why did God have men write the Bible? ______________________
____

THE LANGUAGE OF A STORYTELLER

The Anglo-Saxon language gradually changed. Words were added from Latin and from Norman French. Word endings changed. Vowels within words changed. Old English became Middle English. One of the great writers of the Middle English time was Chaucer. In some of his writings you can see Modern English words.

Geoffrey Chaucer was born about 1340 AD, the son of John and Agnes Chaucer. His last name tells us that his ancestors came from France. Chaucer is a French name that came from the word *chausseur*. *Chausseur* means **cobbler** in French. Originally, the Chaucer family was in the shoemaker trade. Geoffrey's great, great grandparents had moved to England.

Geoffrey was a curious, bright-eyed boy. He lived in London, England, where life was full of new and exciting things. Geoffrey learned many things about the world outside of London as he watched merchant ships come and go. He saw foreign sailors with rings in their ears loading and unloading cargo. He watched his father and other stately merchants buy and sell. Home was a busy place, where servants and guests were always a part of the household. The world was a busy place, **abounding** in interest. Geoffrey was alert and excited about each adventure that a new day could bring.

Geoffrey attended a church school in London. There he learned about the life of a **monk**. He was a good student and learned many things on his own. From his **environment** he learned many lessons about pollution and about evil.

After his early school days he went to work in the royal court. He served as a page to Elizabeth, daughter-in-law of Edward III. He later became a soldier and was captured by the French. He was rescued by King Edward and became one of the king's **squires**.

Geoffrey Chaucer is not remembered for his life as a page, soldier, prisoner, or squire. Many people have had those experiences and have been long forgotten. Geoffrey Chaucer is remembered because he wrote about all the exciting people he met and the events that occurred in his life. He turned his love for life into stories. His stories and poems are masterpieces that people have read and enjoyed for almost six hundred years.

The English language of Chaucer's day was very different from the English language we speak today. His language is referred to as Middle English. The following passage was taken from his most famous poem, *The Canterbury Tales:*

When that Aprille with his shoures soote
The droghte of Marche hath perced to the roote

That passage means this in Modern English:

As soon as April with his showers soft
The drought of March hath pierced to the root...

Compare the Modern English words in Column B with the Middle English words in Column A. Notice how they are alike and how they are different. By comparing the words Chaucer used with words you speak, read, and write, you will see how the language has changed in 500 years.

A	B	A	B
soule	soul	agaynes	against
agayns	again	oure	our
felaweshipe	fellowship	huntying	hunting
gided	guided	wyght	wife
wythoute	without	mayde	maid
housbonde	husband	hym	him
sholde	should	brenne	burn
hir	her	clepe	call
neyther	neither	lessoun	lesson
oughte	ought	lyvynge	living
knyght	knight	synke	sink
ther	there	pleyed	played
smyling	smiling	wolde	would
erly	early	fadre	father
knowynge	knowing		

Complete this activity.

3.6 Translate the short prayer taken from Chaucer's writing into Modern English.

a. There of they thanken oure Lord Jhesu Christ, of whom proceedeth al wit and al goodnesse.

____

____

b. Wherefore I biseke yow mekely, for the mercy of God, that ye preye for me that Christ have mercy on me and forgeve me my giltes.

____

____

____

____

THE ENGLISH LANGUAGE IN AMERICA

Isn't it exciting to know that God brought about changes in language just as He said He would! He confused the language of the people of Babel and scattered the people all over the world. These new languages then began to grow and change. They are still changing today.

People who are moving from one place to another cause language to come into being, change, and grow. Books that tell the history of language agree with this Biblical truth without giving God credit for starting the process.

Modern English. The history of the English language demonstrates God's method of origin and change. Do you remember reading about the Anglo-Saxon tribes who came from Germany and settled in England? The Normans from France conquered the Anglo-Saxons and brought about the change that led to the Middle English language of Chaucer. After that, years of struggle, invasion, and moving around led to Modern English.

When Columbus discovered the New World, he met natives who spoke a language different from his own. When Pilgrims and others came to America, they brought different languages with them. The Pilgrims and the Native Americans had to learn how to communicate with one another. Mixing of the languages occurred, just as it did when the Anglo-Saxons settled together.

North American Indians added words to the English language. Some of these words are pronounced the same way as the Indians pronounced them. Say these words: *maize*, *squash*, *moccasin*, and *Mississippi*. These words were added to the English language when the Pilgrims settled with the North American Indians.

Other European people also came to the New World, and each group added words to the language. The American English language has adopted words from people, inventions, and events. The readiness to adopt words has kept the language changing and growing.

Complete these activities.

3.7 List as many words as you can that have been added to our language since people began to travel in space.

____

____

____

3.8 Name at least three things that influence the growth of any language.

a. ______________________________

b. ______________________________

c. ______________________________

Answer *true* **or** *false.*

3.9 ________ The North American Indians have always spoken the Modern English language.

3.10 ________ The Pilgrims added to a mixture of language in America.

3.11 ________ The North American Indians used words that were added to the English language.

3.12 ________ The people from Holland, France, Germany, and Sweden spoke their own language when they came to America.

3.13 ________ At Babel, God changed language by confusing people's speech and making it impossible for them to understand one another.

3.14 ________ As people moved from place to place, new languages were born.

Time line. The order that events have happened in history can be shown by a *time line.* A time line is easy to use and gives you a quick and useful picture of major events.

Answer the questions about the following time line.

Creation | Man's Fall | Flood | Tower of Babel | The Nation of Israel | Christ's Birth | Death and Resurrection | Church Begins

God's Time Line

3.15 What major event occurred just before the Tower of Babel?

____

3.16 What major event occurred after the Resurrection of Christ?

____

3.17 What exists on both sides of the time line? ____________________

Develop your own time line.

3.18 Use the following events from *The English Language In America.* Put the events in order. Copy the time line on a large paper and illustrate it.

Normans conquer Anglo-Saxons
Pilgrims come to America
Anglo-Saxons settle in England
Other Europeans add words
Indian words are added to English

About A.D. 500	About A.D. 1000	About A.D. 1500 to the present		

Teacher check ____
Initial Date

WORD STUDY

The word study in this section will be about homonyms, idioms, and abbreviations.

Homonyms. Words that sound alike but are spelled differently and have different meanings are called *homonyms.*

Write a homonym for each of the following words.

3.19 altar
________________________ - to change

3.20 ball
________________________ - to cry

3.21 creek
________________________ - to squeak

3.22 flea
________________________ - to run away from

3.23 fur

______________ - a tree

3.24 heel

______________ - to get well

______________ - contraction for *he will*

3.25 horse

______________ - on the way to losing your voice

3.26 miner

______________ - someone under age; insignificant

3.27 ring

______________ - to squeeze dry

3.28 paws

______________ - to stop for a short moment

3.29 sight

______________ - a place on which to build

______________ - to quote someone or something

Write a definition for each homonym.

3.30 bore ______________

boar ______________

3.31 colonel ______________

kernel ______________

3.32 load ______________

lode ______________

3.33 racket ______________

racquet ______________

3.34 stationery ______________

stationary ______________

Idioms. Idioms are phrases that have meanings that cannot be understood from the literal meaning of the words. People who are learning the English language become confused or alarmed when they try to interpret idioms. Consider the following underlined idioms and think about how they could be misunderstood if the listener didn't know how to interpret the phrase.

Bobby was in a jam.
Susan caught a cold.
The family was unable to take in the sights.
Bobby knew this remark would make the fur fly.

Authors use idioms to make their stories interesting and sometimes humorous.

Idioms

Match the idiom with its meaning. Write the letter beside the correct answer on the line.

3.35	______	in a jam	a. made a very great effort to help
3.36	______	got wind of	b. have very few left
3.37	______	catch on	c. in trouble
3.38	______	out of hand	d. decided not to do something
3.39	______	got cold feet	e. heard about
3.40	______	bent over backwards	f. remain calm
3.41	______	uptight	g. get the idea
3.42	______	lost in a book	h. no longer have control over
3.43	______	run short of	i. very interested in a book
3.44	______	stay cool	j. very nervous about something

Complete this activity.

3.45 Write a paragraph using the idioms from the activity you just completed. Underline each idiom as you use it. Use a separate piece of paper.

Teacher check ____

Initial Date

Abbreviations. An abbreviation is a shortened form of a word. A period is put at the end of an abbreviation to signal that the word has been shortened.

Complete these activities.

3.46 Study the following abbreviations. Write the word each represents. If you cannot spell the word, look it up in the dictionary.

a. St. ______	j. Jan. ______	s. Gen. ______
b. Ave. ______	k. Feb. ______	t. Rev. ______
c. Mon. ______	l. Mar. ______	u. Deut. ______
d. Tue. ______	m. Apr. ______	v. Ps. ______
e. Wed. ______	n. Aug. ______	w. Prov. ______
f. Thurs. ______	o. Sept. ______	x. Matt. ______
g. Fri. ______	p. Oct. ______	y. Eph. ______
h. Sat. ______	q. Nov. ______	z. Lev. ______
i. Sun. ______	r. Dec. ______	aa. Col. ______

3.47 Write the word for these abbreviations.

a. c. ______ e. min. ______
b. lg. ______ f. tbs. ______
c. tsp. ______ g. tsp. ______
d. doz. ______

3.48 Write the word for the abbreviations you would find on a travel schedule.

a. lv. ______ b. arr. ______

3.49 Write the word for the abbreviation used for the following directions.

a. N. ______ b. S. ______
c. E. ______ d. W. ______

3.50 Write the word for the abbreviations used for the metric measuring system.

a. kw ______ d. cm ______
b. kg ______ e. dm ______
c. km ______ f. mm ______

Write the vocabulary word for each definition.

3.51 Surroundings that influence growth. ______
3.52 German. ______
3.53 A young man of a noble family who attends to knight. ______
3.54 Man who gives up everything else for religion. ______
3.55 To get involved in. ______
3.56 Harm done in return for a wrong. ______
3.57 Be plentiful. ______
3.58 Expert in judging fine foods. ______
3.59 An Old English poet. ______
3.60 Person who repairs shoes. ______
3.61 Wandering. ______

COMPOSITION

A paragraph is about one topic. It has an introductory sentence, usually three or more detail sentences, and a summary sentence. Keep the following things in mind as you write.

Use *capital letters* to begin the first word of every sentence and to begin all proper nouns.

Use a *period* at the end of each sentence that makes a statement.

Use a *question mark* at the end of each sentence that asks a question.

Use *commas* to separate a series of words or ideas.

Complete this activity.

3.62 Write a descriptive story of at least three paragraphs. Select one of the following topics.

Story topics (these are not titles):

a. First experiences in saying words
b. The most exciting thing I ever heard
c. A good listener
d. When I am told, "No"
e. Thoughts, words, and actions
f. One time I compared

If these topics do not start you writing, think of a new topic about your experience with language.

Teacher check ______________________________
Initial Date

HANDWRITING AND SPELLING

Continue to apply your handwriting and spelling skills to everything you write.

Handwriting. Notice the manner in which the capital letters O, P, R, S, and T are formed.

Complete these handwriting activities.

3.63 Look at the examples and copy them on the following lines.

3.64 Write each of the following words. Use a separate piece of paper.

Ohio
Pennsylvania
Richmond
Sacramento
Texas

Teacher check ______________________________
Initial Date

Spelling. *Antonyms* are words with opposite meanings. In this spelling lesson, you will learn to spell some common antonyms. Continue to use the five-step spelling plan as you learn the words from Spelling Words-3.

Spelling Words-3

admit
advance
attract
casual
compliment
deny
destroy
discourage
encourage
fact
fiction
formal
gush
insult
joyous
preserve
repel
retreat
sorrowful
trickle

Complete this spelling activity.

3.65 Write the spelling words in your best handwriting.

a. ______________________
b. ______________________
c. ______________________
d. ______________________
e. ______________________
f. ______________________
g. ______________________
h. ______________________
i. ______________________
j. ______________________
k. ______________________
l. ______________________
m. ______________________
n. ______________________
o. ______________________
p. ______________________
q. ______________________
r. ______________________
s. ______________________
t. ______________________

Teacher check ______________________________
Initial Date

Match each word with its antonym.

3.66	________	advance	a. formal
3.67	________	attract	b. insult
3.68	________	casual	c. encourage
3.69	________	compliment	d. gush
3.70	________	deny	e. sorrowful
3.71	________	discourage	f. fact
3.72	________	fiction	g. retreat
3.73	________	preserve	h. destroy
3.74	________	joyous	i. admit
3.75	________	trickle	j. repel

Use each pair of antonyms in the following sentences.

3.76 The army was told to a. ______________ but it began to b. ____________ .

3.77 The water would a. ________________________ out of the faucet, so I turned it down to a b. ________________________ .

3.78 The food will a. ________________________ flies, so we need something to b. ________________________ them.

3.79 Our defeat was a a. ________________________ event, but for some reason Bob was b. ________________________ .

3.80 The wedding called for a. ________________________ dress, but Sam wore his b. ________________________ clothes.

3.81 Our government is making an attempt to a. ________________________ the bald eagle, but some people would b. ________________________ it.

3.82 We should a. ________________________ your good work rather than b. ________________________ it.

3.83 The story was strictly a. ________________________ , but some people mistook it for b. ________________________ .

3.84 At first the thief would a. ________________________ that he took anything, then later b. ________________________ it.

3.85 We should a. ________________________ good eating habits rather than b. ________________________ them.

Ask your teacher to give you a practice spelling test of Spelling Words-3. Restudy the words you missed.

SelfTest

Before you take this last Self Test, you may want to do one or more of these self checks.

1. ________ Read the objectives. See if you can do them.
2. ________ Restudy the material related to any objectives that you cannot do.
3. ________ Use the SQ3R study procedure to review the material:
   a. **S**can the sections.
   b. **Q**uestion yourself again.
   c. **R**ead to answer your questions.
   d. **R**ecite the answers to yourself.
   e. **R**eview areas you did not understand.
4. ________ Review all vocabulary words, activities, and Self Tests, writing a correct answer for every wrong answer.

SELF TEST 3

Match the homonym with its definition (each answer, 2 points).

3.01	________	creek	a. to squeak
3.02	________	creak	b. a seed of corn
3.03	________	horse	c. vein of metal ore
3.04	________	hoarse	d. a small stream
3.05	________	colonel	e. on the way to losing your voice
3.06	________	kernel	f. what is being carried
3.07	________	stationery	g. an animal
3.08	________	stationary	h. writing or letter paper
3.09	________	load	i. not moving
3.010	________	lode	j. an army officer

Underline the correct pronunciation for each heteronym (each answer, 3 points).

3.011 The *wind* blew my hat off.
wind wīnd

3.012 Try not to *wind* the spring too tight.
wind wīnd

3.013 Did you *read* your Bible today?
red rēd

3.014 No, but I *read* it yesterday.
red rēd

Add a prefix or suffix to each of the following root words to change or add to its meaning (each answer, 3 points).

3.015	______	ripe	3.021	grace	______
3.016	______	sincere	3.022	end	______
3.017	______	pure	3.023	teach	______
3.018	______	wise	3.024	event	______
3.019	______	perfect	3.025	favor	______
3.020	______	human			

Write the meaning for each of the underlined idioms (each answer, 5 points).

3.026 The boy had <u>butterflies in his stomach</u> as he made his speech.

____

3.027 Don't <u>throw your money away</u> on all that candy.

____

3.028 Father always <u>bends over backwards</u> to help neighbors.

____

3.029 The contest <u>got out of hand</u> when the boys began to fight.

____

3.030 These diamonds are <u>as big as watermelons</u>.

____

Answer the questions about the author's purpose (each answer, 5 points).

3.031 For what purpose are most mystery stories written?

____

3.032 For what purpose did God have men write the Bible?

____

Possible Score	100
My Score	________
Teacher check	________
	Initial Date

Take your spelling test of Spelling Words-3.

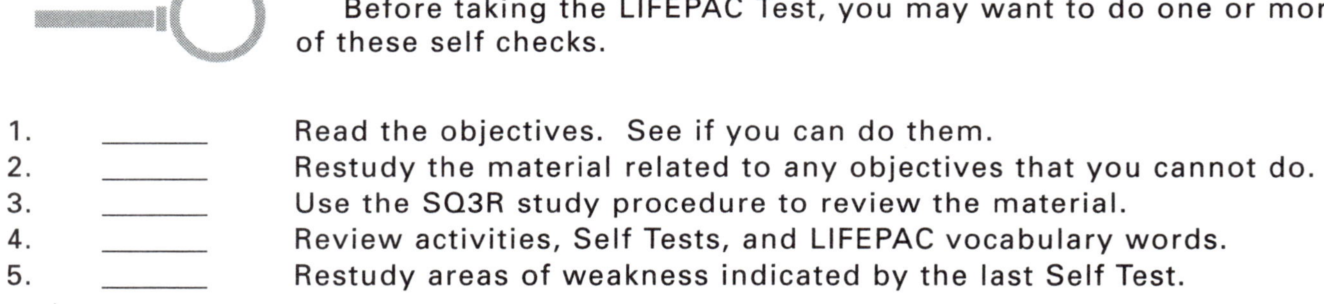

Before taking the LIFEPAC Test, you may want to do one or more of these self checks.

1. ________ Read the objectives. See if you can do them.
2. ________ Restudy the material related to any objectives that you cannot do.
3. ________ Use the SQ3R study procedure to review the material.
4. ________ Review activities, Self Tests, and LIFEPAC vocabulary words.
5. ________ Restudy areas of weakness indicated by the last Self Test.